How to Escape the Trading-Hours-for-Dollars Hamster Wheel

L. Shay Rockhold

www.91DayQuest.com

L. Shay Rockhold

Copyright © 2013 L. Shay Rockhold

All rights reserved.

DEDICATION

To Bill:

*Mentor, cheerleader, best friend, and staunch ally.
I never could have asked for anyone better for those roles.*

W.A.N.

CONTENTS

1. The Background..1
2. The Savvy Six...3
3. Three Options..13
4. The 91 Day Quest System.......................................17
5. Examples..29
6. Conclusion..35
7. Your Next Step..37
8. Resources..39
About the Author..40

Success isn't won. It's designed, planned and pursued.

~ Shay

A FEW NOTES:

- I write the same way that I speak - plainly and clearly. I try to keep my material as simple as possible so that it's easier to follow. It's not all fancy, but it gets the job done.
- This book is designed to be a fairly quick read. (The time consuming part is when you actually put what you read into practice.)
- If you need extra ideas or resources, go to my website. (Check the Resources listed at the end of this book.)
- I don't make any income claims in this book. The amount of money that you make will be dependent on your particular business situation, experience, etc.
- If you have any questions about legal issues, tax issues, etc., you should consult the appropriate authority in those areas. (I am not an attorney, tax professional, etc.)

Don't be afraid to be awesome.

~ Shay

1 THE BACKGROUND

I work with business professionals that already have a pretty strong business. In general, they come to me for help with two different issues:

1. "I would love to take time off, but if I am not seeing clients I am not making any money. I need to get off of the trading-hours-for-dollars hamster wheel."

2. "I would love to spread the word about my business, but I already advertise and use social media. What else can I do?"

Interestingly enough, I help solve both of those problems the same way: by creating additional income streams for the business professional. These income streams not only bring in passive income, but they also let people know about your business.

However, I had a problem.

I have over 60 different income streams that I can help business professionals put into practice. The ones that I suggest will differ depending on what type of business it is and how big the business is, but I can easily implement a different one each week and not use all of them up in a year.

This is good news, right? Well, it is, but I found that

most people are little intimidated by that many options.

So I narrowed it down to six different categories that are applicable to almost every business owner I've worked with and are not complicated to implement.

I call these six different income stream categories "The Savvy Six."

If you take these six categories and realize that there are three different options you have (at a minimum) for each one, that will give you at least 18 different options to use.

This provides a comfortable assortment of options for the average business owner, and it also provides enough flexibility so that a business owner can have diversity in his income, but not be overwhelmed.

(If you're curious about the other income stream possibilities, I cover those in my book *The 91 Day Quest: for a Booming Business.* You can find it on Amazon. Com or on my site.)

In this book I'm going to talk about The Savvy Six, the three different options you can use with each category, the 91 Day Quest System, the P.E.A.R. Method, some examples that you can adapt to your business, and additional resources if you need more help.

2 THE SAVVY SIX

These are the six income stream categories that most business professionals (especially service providers) should not be without.

1. **Newsletters**
2. **Books**
3. **Workshops**
4. **Webinars**
5. **Hotsheets**
6. **Memberships**

When you combine these six categories of income streams along with the three different options for each one that we talk about in the next chapter, you will have *at least* 18 different income streams that you can produce to accompany your main business model.

Intimidating? It shouldn't be.

I'm going to walk you through how to begin implementing these income streams using the **91 Day Quest System** and the **P.E.A.R. Method**.

First let's take a closer look at the Savvy Six:

Newsletters

This is usually one of the first income streams that a business professional will have. At least they will have some semblance of a newsletter, even if it's not exactly effective.

Some professions have generic newsletter services that they can subscribe to to send out to their clients. Some people have lists for their newsletters that they don't even have any control over. Others have no idea what's going on with their newsletters - when they go out, what they look like, what they contain, etc.

When I speak about a business professional having a newsletter, I mean the following:

You have a newsletter service that you personally control, with a customized newsletter that goes out on your schedule and you have some idea of what it contains. You control the content, the frequency, and the list that it goes out to.

Please note that I did not say you had to be the one writing it or sending it out. There is nothing wrong with hiring someone to help you with that, but you need to be in control of it, and you need to at least be in the loop about what is going on with it. The newsletter also can't be a generic one, where the same exact newsletter goes out to 1000 different people in your profession.

If you are sending out the same newsletter that every other person in your industry does, why should a client choose you over someone else? Based on the newsletter you send out, you are just same as everyone else.

Something to think about, isn't it?

Books

I honestly cannot say enough about how important his income stream category is, so I will try to curb my enthusiasm a little bit so that I don't write an entire book (yet) about this one income stream category.

Having a book of your own with you as the author is a tremendous boost for your business.

Not only can you make residual income with royalties, but it's a way to spread the word about your business and to let people know what you do, why you do it, how you do it, and what your personality is like.

It adds authority, credibility, and age certain degree of celebrity when you have your own book (or book series). Having your own book and being a published author open up a multitude of doors that would otherwise be closed for you.

Book signings, press releases, news interviews, and local news features are just a few of the things that are possible when you have your own book.

Another advantage to being a published author is the fact that while your competition is handing out business cards, you can actually hand a book to your prospect. On that book is your name as the author, and if you want to you can put your picture on there, too.

You would be surprised what a difference it makes in the eyes of a prospective client or patient to see your name on a book that you've written.

Not just a book that you had printed yourself at the neighborhood copy store, but an actual book that is available on Amazon.com and through other channels.

I already know what you're thinking, so let me address a few objections that I hear often.

"I hate to write."

There are amazing speech to text software options for you. All you have to do is talk into a microphone and the words will appear on the screen.

Other options would include hiring someone to interview you and turn your interview into a book, or you can turn six months worth of newsletters into a book. Material from your blog can be turned into a book.

Don't let your dislike of writing get in the way of becoming a published author.

"I don't have time."

This is understandable. You already have a business, and you are trying to add something else to your already busy schedule.

You can either carve out 15 or 20 minutes a day in order to work on a book yourself, or you can hire someone else to do it for you.

The important thing to understand is that there are ways for you to hire someone to do it for you while you are still the one who is creating the material for the book. As I mentioned before having a recorded interview edited and turned into a book is a very attractive option.

"I don't know what to write about."

What problems do you see all the time? What mistakes to your clients make before they come to you? What are the questions that you are asked all the time?

Coming up with material for a book is not difficult. In fact, chances are you will have enough material for several books right away (but you just want to work on one at a time).

"It's not really that important, is it?"

Let me answer that by asking you a few other questions.

Are your competitors published authors?

Would having monthly royalty checks deposited in your bank account be a good thing?

Would you like to help people that you may never actually meet face-to-face?

Would you like more people to know about what you're doing?

Would you like for someone to travel 100 miles just to meet you?

Would you like to have an advantage over every single competitor in your area?

Would you like to be able to do workshops or public speaking?

Would you like to be invited to speak to different audiences?

I think you're getting the idea as to how important it is.

There is no excuse for you not to be a published author. You can either take some time and write the book yourself - whether by typing or using a speech to text software program - or you can simply hire someone to help you with it.

Personally, I think it is the best investment than any business professional can make in their business future and their professional career.

Workshops

Workshops are a great way to maximize your time while you spread your message.

Instead of sharing your message one-on-one, you can speak to groups of 20 (or more) at a time.

Chances are that some of the people in your workshop will become clients or customers, but it's very possible that you will make more money per hour by presenting to a group rather than to individuals.

Workshops are especially effective in the health, wellness, fitness, and weight loss fields because there is such a wealth of information that you can present and there is such a need for the information.

If you record your workshops, you can package them up and have them available for sale - and in doing so you can create passive income from your workshops.

Webinars

Similar to workshops, but they are done online instead of in person.

There are a number of platforms that you can use for webinars - such as anymeeting.com or GoToMeeting.com - and both of these will allow you to record your webinars so that you can download them or have them available for people to follow a link and view the webinars at a future date.

Hotsheets

People are looking for information, and sometimes having a quick reference report is better than having an elaborate book or long video.

Hotsheets can help solve specific problems quickly and easily.

The formula that I use for Hotsheets is the following:

"One problem, one solution, 20 pages or less."

These work especially well if you have a business where people ask a number of specific questions over and over.

Each question (and the solution/answer[s]) could be the topic for a new Hotsheet.

Memberships

Memberships can take a number of different forms, but they have the same general concepts.

They are often used either to promote a sense of community, provide ongoing support, or to deliver a stream of information.

You can have memberships that have information

delivered via email, memberships that are based on forums, or memberships that are delivered via a blog format.

The platform you use will depend on the purpose of your membership, and also whether or not you want to have individual members communicate with each other.

Any business can be ideal if you take the time to define it and design it.

~ Shay

3 THREE OPTIONS

For each income stream category, you have three different options that you can use.

Free – Paid - Premium

When I use these terms, I refer to the cost for your prospect or client, not for you.

Free - this is pretty self-explanatory. The most common way you will see this option is when a business offers a free newsletter, and sometimes a free workshop or webinar.

Memberships can be free, as well.

You can even offer your books for free if you want to use them like a big business card or as a freemium offer. Your books can be a wonderful introduction to a prospect, and you will get loads of credibility by sending them a free copy of your book. Free books can be sent for reviews, along with press releases, and a host of other marketing ways.

Paid - when I use the term "paid" in this context, I am referring to the low cost/high-volume model. An example would be a newsletter that only costs five or $10 a month. It's a low-cost, but you make up for it in volume.

Premium - this is an income stream that uses a higher cost/lower volume business model.

Advanced workshops, detailed webinars, newsletters filled with exclusive information, books that have lots of details or are manuals - all of these are examples for a premium business model.

You can always start with a free option and later offer a paid and premium tier.

If you have a book, you can offer a workbook for a higher price, for example. For newsletters, you're free version can have some very basic information and maybe even some advertising, while your paid and premium versions will have more specific information and will probably be advertising free.

Another common option would be to have a free workshop, paid workshops, and premium advanced workshops - think of them as 101, 201 and graduate level college courses. They all build on each other, but they all have different degrees of information and involvement.

If you combine the income stream categories with having three options you can use for each one, you are looking at a minimum of 18 different options.

Notes

Notes

4 THE 91 DAY QUEST SYSTEM

The underlying premise of the 91 Day Quest System is that you can design your ideal business – balanced, booming, and burnout-proof - if you take it 91 days at a time and strategically plan the way you will design your business.

Each Quest is like a piece in the lifelong puzzle of your business. You will get closer and closer to the ideal business with each Quest you take.

Each Quest is 91 days, which is perfect for business because it is the same amount of time as a business quarter.

Once you complete one Quest, you will begin another Quest - just like businesses don't quit their business after only one or two quarters.

With your Quests you have a number of options.

- Work on your own.
- Participating in group coaching
- kicking off your quest with a webinar or workshop and then working on your own
- One-on-one coaching
- Having everything done for you

What you choose will be dependent on what your budget is, how much time you have available, and what you feel comfortable doing.

You can learn more about this in the Resources section.

The P.E.A.R. Method

The basic method that I teach for Quests is the P.E.A.R. Method:

- **Plan**
- **Execute**
- **Assess**
- **Repeat**

You can use this for any Quest - whether it is for business or for your own personal goals.

But if you are pursuing a Quest that is specifically designing your income streams, I modify that method a bit:

Plan – Create – Polish – Publish – Promote

Assess - Repeat

The same basic steps are there, but the "Execute" part is expanded.

This helps to give my clients a bit more structure when they are creating their income streams, and it helps them to develop a more structured time frame for each step.

Once you have completed your first Quest, the "Assess" step is actually part of the "Plan" step in your next Quest. For your first Quest, you will do nothing but planning for your first week because you won't have anything that you need to assess (except perhaps assessing what your business looks like now, and what you've used before now).

Now let's take a look at each step and the time frame you should use for each.

Plan (Week 1)

Your first week is going to be strictly for planning.

You are going to decide which income streams you are going to create. (Category and Option)

Do not create more than three income streams for each Quest. Why? Because if you try to do too much at once, you won't do any of them well.

Another tip: if you are working on a book as one of your income streams, don't try to do three books at once for a Quest. Choose a book and then two other types of income streams.

You are going to check out what your competition is doing during the first week, as well. If your competition is doing workshops, you may not want to do the same thing. Perhaps you could focus on webinars.

The reason why you want to do something different than what your competition is doing is because an added benefit for creating your income streams is that it will also help you beat your competition if it is done correctly. (We'll talk more about that under "Promote.")

Part of the planning process is also deciding when you are going to fit time for your Quest around your already busy schedule. My suggestion is to give yourself at least 30 minutes a day to work on your Quest. This doesn't have to be 30 minutes all at one sitting. You can break that up into two or three short sessions a day, but I would suggest at least 30 minutes a day, five days a week at a minimum.

Notes

Create (Weeks 2-5)

Now that you have decided what you are going to do, it's time to start creating your income streams.

This is when you are going to write your manuscript for your book, create the content for your newsletters, develop the content for your webinars or workshops, etc.

Don't worry so much about making everything perfect at this point. You will be able to go back and polish what you have written and created later. Your main goal is to get all of your content written down and organize your thoughts so that you can be ready for the next part of your Quest.

Notes

_____
_____
_____
_____
_____
_____
_____
_____
_____
_____
_____
_____
_____

Polish (Weeks 6 & 7)

Here is where you're going to make everything look pretty. Revise your work, edit your work, make sure that your "voice" comes through clearly in your writing.

If you need help with the editing, or if you simply need a second opinion, this is where you can ask people to look at what you've done and provide feedback (or you can hire someone to do the editing for you).

This is a great time to show some of your current clients what you have in the works and let them know what's in store. Your clients are a wealth of information, and if you have some that you feel will give you honest feedback on what you have planned, this is the best time to get them involved.

Note that I said *some* and not *all*. This isn't the time to announce what your project is - that will come in the publishing and promoting phases - but this is the time where you can have a few close advocates to take a look at what you're doing.

Notes

_____
_____
_____
_____
_____

Notes

Publish (Weeks 8 & 9)

Now that you have everything the way that you want it, it's time for publishing.

Publishing can mean that you are ready to get your book ready to be published, but it also can mean that your workshops are ready to be promoted and so they have been uploaded and are ready for you to take action. It can mean that your Hotsheets are ready to be sold and they have been loaded into your digital sales and delivery system. It can mean that your newsletters are ready and they have been loaded into the autoresponder.

Whatever you have created, this is the time when you prepare it to be launched on whatever platform you have chosen to do so.

Notes

Promote (Weeks 10–13)

Now that you have your income streams ready, it's time to tell the world about them.

The first-place you need to start is with your current clients, current business associates, plus your friends and family.

You're also going to incorporate your new income streams into any advertising and/or marketing that you're currently doing. Are you running ads? Be sure to mention that you're a published author in your ads. Do you already have a mailing list? Be sure to announce that you have workshops or a new book available.

Whatever you are currently doing, you want to make sure that you are promoting your new ventures along with your main business model.

Why?

There are a number of reasons, but I will start with two:

1. How would your profits increased if half of your clients spent an extra $10 or $20 with you? Right now it may not seem like a big deal, but if you have 100 people spending an extra $20 with you every month, that's an extra $2000. And it's for work you did once and you'll get paid for it over and over.

2. You may have people that will not purchase

your main business offering, but they would be more than willing to spend $10 or $20 with you to learn more about what you do and to get some help with whatever you offer a solution for.

If you are already running an ad, do you understand how many people will do a search for you if you mention in that ad that you have a book out?

A lot more than you think would, to be honest. If you are a chiropractor and you are already running ads (that are effective, of course, or you hopefully wouldn't be running them), and you mentioned in there that you are the author of *Happy Spine, Healthy Times* (or whatever – that's a silly title, but you get the idea), you would be amazed at how many people would do a search for that book just to check it out.

And when they find out that you really are a published author, some of them will buy the book. Others will do business with you just because of the fact that you now have become much more credible in their eyes.

The same thing can be accomplished with your other income streams as well, but I have noticed that becoming a published author puts you in a league by yourself in the eyes of many people in the eyes of many people.

You can use your income streams to help promote your business.

One thing that I do is I will actually send one of my books to prospects before I have an appointment with them. It helps give them an idea of what I do, and it helps them feel like they know me already my the time I talk with them on the phone or they stop by my office.

You can send out invitations to one of your workshops, make offers for your webinars, and much more.

The good thing about your income streams is it is a way for people to get to know you better without making the commitment of being a client. However, many of the people who buy your books, attend your workshops, etc., will end up being your clients because they have had the opportunity of getting to know you and your business better.

Notes

Notes

5 EXAMPLES

I am going to give three examples of how you can fit your income streams together, using three different industries.

By reading through these examples, you should be able to adapt them to fit your business. Be sure to read this with pen and paper in hand so that you can make notes about how you can adapt these examples to your own business.

(Please note that real client names are not used in these examples, and some of these are composites.)

John – Fitness Instructor

- Book
- Free Workshop
- Paid Workshop

John has a thriving business. In fact, that's the main problem that he has - he's working himself to a frazzle trying to deal with seeing clients six days a week.

For his initial Quest he decided to focus on creating a book and two different types of workshops.

Because he has great advice and experience with helping people to lose weight and also get in better shape, he had plenty of material for a book. He also used some of the information for a free workshop, and more advanced information for the paid workshop.

He used the free workshop as an introduction to his services, and also used the paid workshop as well.

But there was another step that he included to help free him from the trading hours for dollars hamster wheel.

In his workshops he promoted his book, and in his free workshops he promoted his paid workshops. The paid workshops and the book focused on how people could become more fit and use his techniques on their own instead of needing him for a personal trainer.

Some people still wanted to hire him personally, but in changing his business model he could work with the clients that he wanted to work with for a premium rate and have other income coming in with the books and workshops.

If he wanted to expand on his Quest, he could add more books, memberships, webinars, and more.

Marie – Life Coach

- Book
- Paid Workshop
- Membership

As with John, Marie had plenty of material for a book. The main difference from John is that Marie used the success stories of previous clients (names and details changed, of course) for the material of her book. She also interlaced her own personal advice within the stories so that someone reading the book could work on their own situation.

Marie decided that free workshops were not something that she wanted to do, so she focused on creating a paid workshop with a similar goal to John: to help more people and be more selective with who she works with one on one.

She also offered an online membership that people could subscribe to for monthly advice, tips, and access to her coaching forum.

She can always expand upon this Quest by adding a premium tier for her membership, more books, premium workshops, and more.

Shawn – Nutritionist

- Book
- Paid Newsletter and membership
- Free Webinars

One of the things that I love about working with people in the health and wellness industry is that there is such a wealth of information that professionals in these fields have to draw upon. They never seem to have any problems creating a number of different income streams because they have so much content that is available to them.

Like the previous examples, Shawn chose to move into the business model of serving more people in a general way and in groups, and choosing to work with fewer people one on one.

Another component is that Shawn decided to place a greater emphasis on transitioning to an online business model instead of working with people in person. This provides a greater flexibility because you are not limited to your geographic area if you choose to work this kind of a business model.

The webinars were free, and in the webinars Shawn promoted his books and newsletters. He briefly mentioned working one-on-one with people, but the emphasis was on how to get ongoing online help.

Normally I would only want someone to work three new income streams per Quest, but in this case someone had so much material that there was very little creation involved - it was mostly reformatting information in order to fit the business platform (book, membership, etc.).

I hope that by now your mind is spinning with possibilities about your own business. I also hope that you been jotting down notes so that you're ready to go with your own Quest.

Notes

L. Shay Rockhold
Notes

6 CONCLUSION

If you are caught on the trading hours for dollars hamster wheel, you are not alone. It is a trap that many business professionals find themselves in, and it is a common source of stress and burnout.

You can take steps to escape this dilemma, starting today.

Design your ideal business, 91 days at a time, by going on your 91 Day Quest.

7 YOUR NEXT STEP

Now you have a choice to make.

- **Do nothing** – this is certainly an option. Just keep doing what you've been doing.

- **Do it yourself** – you might want to get more books, workbooks, workshops, etc., but you do everything yourself with no interactive guidance from me.

- **Group coaching** – you do the work yourself, but I'll be available for feedback via group sessions (conference calls, forum, email, webinars, etc.)

- **One-on-one coaching** – you do the work, but I am working with you on a personal basis with emails and weekly one-on-one calls.

- **Done for you** – I'll touch base with you for information gathering and other reasons, but I'll do all of the actual work.

I only take on one client per industry, per city (or ZIP code).

Contact me (info is on my website – www.91DayQuest.com) for my availability.

You can also check my site to get information about other resources.

L. Shay Rockhold

8 RESOURCES

If you would like to have information about my

- books and workbooks
- workshops
- webinars
- newsletter
- coaching (group or 1 on 1)
- and more

please visit my website: **www.91DayQuest.com**

If you would like to have income streams created for you, you can contact me via my site. My phone number is on there, and there is also a contact form.

Here are some tools that will help you with your Quest:

- Dragon NaturallySpeaking - a speech to text tool. Speak to the microphone and your words appear on the page.

- GetResponse - this is an auto responder that you can use for your newsletters. There are plenty of tutorials on the site getresponse.com.

ABOUT THE AUTHOR

Shay Rockhold is a business consultant and a Quest Coach. She lives in Charleston, South Carolina.

Her specialty is helping business professionals who are trapped in the vicious cycle of needing to trade hours for dollars escape from the stress and burnout from that business model.

She is a business leader. She leads a local group of over 400 business professionals and she also has online business groups that number near 1000 business owners.

She is also an author, public speaker, mom of three, coffee lover, science-fiction fan, and a Quest Queen.

In addition to using the 91 Day Quest System for her business and her clients, she has used the same approach to lose almost 60 pounds at the time of this writing.